CW00497834

Ed Sanders's great document is gen all investigation. It reclaims powe "'istorin", as scrappy yet sophist._____, _____, adventure. Investigate the Abyss! perfect rallying cry for the Kali Yuga mess we're in. Data as sanity, as earth-touching mudra to awakened mind. Down with cognitive dissonance! Key scripture to Jack Kerouac School Naropa's pedagogy since early inception, Investigative Poetics holds ground in this elegant new edition with elucidating preface by Don Byrd. Long live the cultural intervention this text already was and continues to be. Facing ethical and ecological crisis and loss of historical memory and dynastic corporate control and greed, we needed Sanders's IP anew and available. It is powerful apotropaic medicine to the syndicates of samsara, a tool kit for survival, mind and senses in tact. And as brilliant antidote to distraction culture, you can actually wake up in the morning and DO something!

We had early heady days at Naropa in Boulder Colorado, close to the great divide, and negative ions, and east & west sympathies and symmetries, and eidolons of TAZ and rhizome and icons and scions of the New American Poetry converging to test their mettle and imagination with one another, with horrors of Viet Nam barely over, sixties burnout, New Contract with America on horizon. We know the rest. During our protests at Rocky Flats, Allen Ginsberg wrote his doc-po "Plutonian Ode" I think influenced by Ed's method. We all knew how useful Ed's ideas were and carried them with us to other places and into the work as well. Some of the energy for my own obsession with archive come to mind, as well as the trickle down to field poets everywhere.

Anne Waldman

....one of the most important documents, texts, textbooks, and manifestos or manifestations to come into my hands since—I guess it's the most important thing for me since "Projective Verse" itself.

George Butterick

Ed Sanders' clarion call is for American poets—in a paranoid time when poems, "news that stays news," get accused of false news—"to resume their ancient tradition of describing historical reality." The methodology he proposed in the 1975 "Investigative Poetry" lectures has already bequeathed to us, with Sanders' Lucan-like facility for poetry and scholarship, a quarter century of multi-volume verse histories. The advance of *Investigative Poetry* laps the formal innovation of "a poem including history" even as it answers Olson's consuming desire to establish a methodology. Sanders asserts that the long-poem is history. That poetry is the language of history. That our great poets (he names in the first few pages Pound, Crane, Williams, Olson, Ginsberg, Snyder, Rothenberg, d.a. levy) begin as scholars of primary sources. That the poem is a sharp instrument for investigating the era. A poem on the order of *De Incendio Urbis* is a threat to the despots of any era and all eras. Sanders' contemporary masters Sebald and Bolaño, lacking native histories of *Investigative Poetry*, nevertheless were moved to carry out detective work in prose fictions.

move over Herodotus
move over Thuc'
move over Arthur Schlesinger
move over logographers and chroniclers
and compulsive investigators

for the poets are
marching again
upon the hills
of history

Rich Blevins

A sense of victory in remaining embedded/embodied in/ as the-book-the-bard. Rather than useless "forgetful symbols"—transitory moments that pass on us or pass us by or pass along—it is from the stance of integrities of our involvement where we create bridges to future bards. "Sweet nets of bard-babble"—permission to speak freely. In the invitation, "you make law" by "concomitant chords." Freedom to create, I most appreciate the encouragement to keep going beyond the threat of being stopped—no matter how seemingly rich or convincing or historical that threat may be believed to be.

    j/j hastain

Some of us had the fortune of discovering Ed Sanders' *Investigative Poetry* at our beginnings. For me it was the birth of the poet after many aborted efforts and has remained a major root. Sanders and the Fugs' incantation to exorcise and levitate the Pentagon at the height of the Vietnam War, his coverage for the LA Times of the trial of Charles Manson and subsequent, extraordinary book, *The Family*, and his essay, *Investigative Poetry*, are the root of a whole generation of poets. With Dispatches' much needed reprint here it will become a root for generations of poets to come.

    Sharon Doubiago

INVESTIGATIVE POETRY

ED SANDERS

WITH AN INTRODUCTORY ESSAY TO THE NEW EDITION BY
DON BYRD

never again
to internalize
grovelness

Dispatches   Editions

Roots & Branches Series

Library of Congress Cataloging in Publication Data

Sanders, Ed. Investigative poetry. A lecture prepared for the Visiting
Spontaneous Poetics Academy of the Naropa Institute in Boulder, Colo.,
in the summer of 1975.
1. American poetry—20th century—History and criticism—Addresses,
essays, lectures.
2. History in literature.
I. Title. PS323.5S2   811' .5'0931   76-892

INVESTIGATIVE POETRY: THE DOSSIER, 2018

DON BYRD

The Fugs:
"I said, 'Hello to the grief bird…, hello grief bird, what's happening?'"

Maya Thompson (age 6):
"The roller coasters are all broken. The lollipops are all eaten." (2016)

Edward Snowden to Laura Poitras:
"Assume that your adversary is capable of a trillion guesses per second."

Is it possible to state the extremity of the Earthly condition
without sounding like a crank or an hysteric?

Charles Olson, in *Maximus IV, V, VI*: "the societal / is an undeclared war"—now more declared than otherwise. The thugs used to hide behind operations with the appearance of legitimacy—the military, the banks, construction companies, county boards, and such. The scholarly thugs hid behind traditional academic disciplines. The most vulgar and money-grubbing criminal element has now made a brazen and mostly successful world-wide grab for power. Olson foresaw this change as early as1945 when he refused to take the high government position that was the due plum for his work in the 1944 Presidential campaign. The crooks of the Pendergast gang from Kansas City who peopled the Truman administration were early warning signs.

The humans interpreted the meager data available to them in terms of the universal and reductive pattern of the ancient Tradition. It was this oppressive form that Sanders challenged in *Investigative Poetry. Now the data have become the pattern—the many patterns incohering together. This changes everything. We are now in the crisis of the opportunity that Ed recognized more than forty years ago.*

The humans were forever beginning again. They would return collectively to the lonely, solipsistic human soul and the cosmos—the difference that was the same—seeking renewed focus. The available data at most gave a hint of Earthly constraints and forms. The Chaldean astronomers noted the precession of the equinoxes, and their data were studied and revised as evidence that the patterns of cosmic change belonged to larger patterns of cosmic stability until the time of Brahe and Kepler. For almost three millennia, this trivial pattern, selected from endless, possible patterns, was about the only effective data. Appearing to underwrite far more harmony and meaning than it justified, it was taken as the form of cosmology and the form of human personality. Otherwise there were habits of behavior, rules of thumb, and tautologies.

It was only when the production of data began to spill over that things got interesting. Malthus based a generalized demographic theory on a little data sent back to England from the imperial bureaucrats. A few pages of notes on the beaks of finches in the Galapagos Islands punched a hole in the scientific-philosophic tradition that still has not been repaired. Physics, molecular biology, and the philosophy of history—all of the formal disciplines really—still deal in a universal medium that binds time and treats the flow of life as an illusion. It was not until after World War II that data could be measured, organized, and processed in significant amounts. The first studies of economics that were based on significant amounts of data appeared shortly before the Trump administration declared data to be of no interest.

Sometime toward the end of the last century, ideas were decoupled from the media and machinery of knowing. Daniel Hillis called this the moment of "functional abstraction." Ideas do not just represent states of the machine, they function; they do something. There is no universal medium. There is no technology. The techno-logos no more exists than the Word that was in the beginning. The abstract machines do not replicate their origin. Abstract machines that refer to less abstract things, such as their own media, create maddening loops and paradoxes. Abstract machines refer properly to their consequences. The data site is the place of prophecy and choice. Prophecy is effective not because the future is foreseen, but because it is made. The Earth is the work of poetry. Think about this. Whole worlds tumble down on this thought.

Ed Sanders was almost alone in noticing that something big was up.

Investigative Poetry was prophetic and mostly ignored. Only now, the election of 2016 has energized something of the kind of investigation that Sanders imagined. The Twitter feed of the poet Seth Abramson (@sethabramson) is exemplary. Investigators for the now obsolete newspapers and bright, mostly young investigators working for net sites with odd names like Buzz Feed and the Daily Beast do labor-intensive research, spending long, boring hours in hangouts around the seats of power, and, when they score some data that have consequences for the developing narrative, they appear as talking heads on cable news. The new spectator sport, however, is strange: MSNBC and Fox News, although they compete fiercely, play different games. Fox deploys no investigators. The political parties now are DATA and NO DATA.

*   *   *

In a flawed but important poem near the beginning of the third volume of the *Maximus,* Olson refers to Cardinal Richelieu, who developed and promoted important ideas behind the modern nation state and the surveillance state, as "The last man / except the Soviets—or Mao when he was / living in the Yenan Cave community." The humanist image of the singular man and the image of the collective man were flip sides of the universal man.

The HumOS is an abstract machine that represents itself as an image of *all possible things, including itself.* Men (and weirdly women) are examples of Man. Everything, not including Man, but weirdly *also* including man, is an example of the World or universe or the generalized One. There is a nervous jitter at the center of the human data site. Man and World flip back and forth like an optical illusion. The vase is two faces (it is an image of set theory). *Things exist* because they are examples of other things or of things that do not exist at all—Ideas, essences, metaphysical coinage. *Things are true* because they are parts of the generalized "truth" that can be exchanged for other parts (words for things, dollars for donuts, and so forth). *There is something fishy about this.*

In the beginning, a distinction was drawn: heaven was distinguished from earth, the (empty) *cogito* was distinguished from the (empty) cognized space. This is an unthinkable sloppiness. All of the paradigms produced the same world, with the same lonely solipsist and the same cruel, generalizing god (or nature or global economy) at the center. This universal three-in-oneness / one-in-threeness inherited from primitive mythology prevailed from the Pythagorean family romance, which Plato appropriated in the *Timaeus*, through Stoic logic, which dwelt upon and thoroughly investigated the third place, the Augustinian trinity, the mediating thirds of the Cartesian pineal gland and the Kantian categories, the dialectical thirds of Hegelian and Marxian theory, the family threesome of psychoanalysis, the ontological triunity of Peirce and the early cyberneticists, Lacan's triadic imaginary, symbolic, and real, as well as the prolific multiplicities of current vitalist and biopolitical philosophies of language, which, though they subvert their own settlement into triadic unity, delineate themselves as possible thirds and circle the absent unity as the geese in the myth circled the sunken Atlantis. *These were all attempts to solve the equation of the Many that are One.*

The mysterious thing-unthing that unified the human world and the HumOS was not just a theoretical object; it was the Nut of the World Tree—the most general and abstract of things. It manifested as an idol or a sacred grove or holy chapel, a song or some thing, the original nature of which was forgotten—just the sacred old whatever, a shapeless piece of leather or an oddly-shaped log. These were pulled out of the church and danced around the town square on the holiday. People without a theoretical or philosophic twitch in their bodies lived and breathed the generalized images that were both themselves and their world or mommapoppa or Nature or the image of god, perhaps god himself. The weird object was simple for simple people, but—and this is the amazing fact—the simple Nut functioned in its simplicity exactly like the Nut of the gravest and most learned philosophers.

One, two, three; one, two, three. It was waltz time, "the moving image of eternity" (the phrase, probably the most quoted in the philosophic literature, is from the *Timaeus*); it moved and flipped on all scales from subatomic to cosmic. *Toward the end of the last century, evolving complex intelligence began to count in earnest: "One, two, three, four, five.... This was new. This was the opening of abstract expressionism, projective poetry and free jazz. The matter-energy site gave way to the matter-energy-information site. The HumOS had never provided a way for the Earth to be known.*

In *Investigative Poetry*, Ed Sanders proposes to take the situation in hand. As a celebrity among the celebrities when data celebrity was a new thing, he knew first-hand the waves of information and their fragility. Sanders knew what the deepest theorists of information did not clearly articulate for twenty-five years: data is a function of time.

> Files age
> Files wax rusty
> The data corrodes
> by the tendency of
> poets to escape into
> the symbols.

To escape into the symbols is what it means to live in a normative world—the generalized human world, in which everything is either an example or an allegorical figure beyond life and death. We blew through 1984 and the imagination of total control on the first wave of this newness. Large populations can be controlled by huge allotments of entertainment, apparent freedom, and moments of unexpected or selective repression, arbitrary inequalities, and random killings.

The Many that were One became the many that were more.

The virtual humans do not look like their selfies. Don't tell them.

*   *   *

In 1976 Sanders had a smell of the collusion that has now come into the open and has revealed its barbarity. Power in the 1970s was tidy, genteel, and murderous. From *The Z-D Generation*:

> William Colby is probably
> a Russian mole. You laugh! But
>   in a way many of them
>   in the War Caste
>   were Russian Moles:

loving the up-tight Russian mode
of repression, aping the KGB, loving
the thrill of control and
surveillance.

William Colby was a career American intelligence agent, a colleague called him a "soldier priest." Beginning during World War II, he worked with the resistance movements in occupied Europe and rose through the ranks to be the Director of Central Intelligence from 1973 to 1976 under Presidents Nixon and Ford. Spies are inherently double agents. They must exchange what at least appears to be real information for what they get in return. An article in this morning's paper questions whether Carter Page was a Russian spy or an American spy.

The CIA hardliners, and others, had reasons to question Colby. Under, James R. Schlesinger, Colby's predecessor as Director, Colby had carried out an internal investigation of illegal activities and misconduct during the CIA's early and mostly uncontrolled years. He revealed shocking programs: 'Operation Mockingbird,' which spread fake news in the American media; 'Operation Phoenix,' a program that assassinated North Vietnamese agents in the South on a massive scale; attempts to assassinate Fidel Castro; and experiments with LSD on unwitting human subjects. Colby himself, before becoming CIA Director, oversaw Operation Phoenix. He died under mysterious circumstances twenty years after he left the CIA. Conspiracy theories have circulated. Many people believe that he finally paid his dues to one of several possible sides.

John Jesus Angleton was one of the CIA insiders who believed Colby was a Russian mole. It is not surprising that Angleton was paranoid. One of his best friends, Harold (Kim) Philby, turned out to be a notorious Soviet spy and defected. At Yale Angleton had been a student of Maynard Mack, the literary theorist and proponent of New Criticism, and Norman Holmes Pearson, one of the founders of American Studies, literary executor of Hilda Doolittle, and an American espionage agent and CIA recruiter. Angleton was a poet and, with Reed Wittemore, published the Yale magazine *Furioso*, which published e.e. cummings,

Ezra Pound, and William Carlos Williams. Angleton was a friend of William Buckley and corresponded with Pound and Eliot.

Richard Helms, CIA Director under Johnson and Nixon, said, "Jim was recognized as the dominant counterintelligence figure in the non-communist world." When Colby fired Angleton in 1975, it was found that his program had personal files on two million Americans and that, in collusion with the Post Office, it had opened and photographed 200,000 or more letters. Angleton was instrumental in hiring students from the Yale English Department because, he believed, people trained in New Criticism and close literary analysis had the ideal skill set to be spies. (The 2006 spy film, *The Good Shepherd*, is based vaguely on Angleton's story.)

February 2, 2018. The relatively stable authoritarianism of 1975, based on factual investigation and coherent policy, has now given way to the authoritarianism of chaos and randomness. Much of the power, wealth, and information is hidden. If one applies the techniques of close reading and deep analysis of New Criticism to the data site now, one surely arrives at the conclusion that the textual fabric is mostly random.

Donald Trump is probably a Russian mole. Or he is an unconscious asset of several conflicting handlers. He managed to turn a substantial inheritance and creative hype into celebrity and inexhaustible lines of credit. He is an exemplary figure in the conversion of capitalism into debtism. He appears to be paying debts with his Presidency. About 2003, after repeated bankruptcies, American banks became reluctant to underwrite his dubious projects. He undertook numerous hucksterish and fraudulent business schemes—selling steaks, wines, and licenses to market his brand name. The so-called Trump University was clearly fraudulent, and he finally settled the outstanding suits for $25 million after he was already well into the Presidential campaign. Much of his 'success' in real estates in recent years, mostly selling condos in New York City, has the overwhelming smell of laundering Russian black money.

The deep structure of the visible chaos is invisible chaos. Occasionally, there is a glimpse into the almost comic depths of the data site. Thus, Glenn Simpson in testimony on the Steele dossier before the House Intelligence Committee (11-8-17): *"So there was a gangster—a Russian gangster living in Trump Tower.... His gangster name is Taiwanchik.... he was running a high-stake gambling ring out of Trump Tower, while he himself was a fugitive for having rigged the skating competition at the Salt Lake Olympics.... And when Mr. Trump went to the Miss Universe pageant in 2013, Taiwanchik was there in the VIP section with Mr. Trump and lots of other Kremlin biggies."* (Edited for clarity and brevity)

Trump is a generator of instability, fear, and anger, which, along with the crassest forms of venality, are the sources of his power. He is not the master of the chaotic data site (it has no master) but its public face and the clown of a virtual world where there is no authentic existence and no viable system of truth. Authentic existence and viable truth, however, are secondary. *Investigative poetry constructs sites of meaning and value on which existence and truth are powerful measures.*

*   *   *

It began to be noted in the 1950s that there was another physical component of Earthly organization. There were the fundamental matter-energy forces, which, as they did not seem to belong to a unified system, were at the center of research in physics, and there was information. Information was a new quantity that raised formal questions of a new and different order. Matter and energy follow the conservation laws. The log can be burned in the fireplace and warm the room. The energy that is stored in the log is released and distributed equally throughout the system. The energy is conserved, but the warmth is lost. Classical physics does not account for warmth, which is dismissed as an accidental consequence or the event of the conversion of matter and energy.

Information is warmth. The heating up of the Earth is not merely a matter of CO_2 emissions and average global temperatures, it is the burning of a civilization that understands its mechanisms in terms of existence and truth, rather than meaning and value. "Alchemists & cooks have the same problem, how to manage the heat' (Gerrit Lansing in "Burden of Set"). Alchemy was the first information science. This is the reason Bacon and Newton were interested in it. Nothing happens in the matter-energy world. Alchemy was the best available accounting of time and transformation, meaning and value. Bacon's and Newton's intuition still has not been solidly articulated and implemented.

Alchemy was the complement of tragedy. The bards of old were tragic creatures, for whom death was the aim and justification of life. Olson tried to find the prophecy of another life in the innocence of characters in Shakespeare's (alchemical) tragicomedies. Sanders quotes Ginsberg: *"now is the time of prophecy without death as a consequence." The practice of investigative poetry is addressed not to the deathliness of existence and truth, which are mechanisms of entropy—useful to know about, albeit not fundamental—but to action in time and the creation of possibilities:*

RELENTLESS
PURSUIT OF DATA:

Interrogate the abyss

. . .

To surround an item of time
with thick vector-clustors
Gnosis ....

The traces of the world that was our mythical origin were erased in the labor-intensive investigations that got us here. In one of the most important books of the last fifty years (and almost entirely ignored), *The Mathematical Theory of Information* (2002), Jan Kåhre writes: "...a real system which cannot forget is beyond theory. Biological evolution proceeds by the elimination of history: by random variation (divergence) and by selection (convergence).... Erasure is a precondition for evolution." Kåhre defines information as that component of the physical data site that interacts with matter and energy, but is overwritten, used up, and disappears. Its advantage is that it can also be created from nothing. *Information is life and warmth.*

What can the grief bird say? The first mass-produced computer, the IBM 360 and its numerous peripherals, which appeared in 1965, cost $1.37 million and weighed about 6 tons. It is difficult to compare specs directly because the terminology has changed, but as a computing machine, it was not comparable in computing power and use to the billions of smart phones of 2018.

Toward the end of the last century, Earth people begin to communicate with one another and with the dynamic forms of the Earth. Information was produced in prodigious amounts. This has happened since the publication of *Investigative Poetry*. It was estimated in 2000 that, if all human communications before the appearance of digital technology were transcribed and digitized, it would amount to about 5 Exabytes of data (an Exabyte being a billion gigabytes). At that time, roughly 1-2 Exabytes of new data were being created annually. More information was being produced in three or so years than in the entire previous history, and the amounts were accelerating at a stunning rate. The same researchers estimated that 5 Exabytes of data were produced in 2002. By 2016 the U.S. alone produced 2,657,700 gigabytes of Internet data every minute or nearly 4 exabytes a day.

The graph of information production was more or less flat for millennia. There were upward bumps in the Fifth and Twelfth Centuries and the Renaissance. The new data of those moments of intense cultural creativity were powerful but generalized and, by twenty-first century standards, quantitatively trivial. The hyperbolic function that describes the productivity of complex, Earthly intelligence, harbored a surprise—a rare thing in mathematics. The graph that had been relatively flat turned almost straight upward, making an L-shape or a hockey stick. Many forms of Earthly production—information, population, wealth, CO_2 emissions, and so forth—followed the same vertiginous path. Flipped over, the L-shaped graph describes the exhaustion of Earthly resources. Mathematicians had long thought it strange that the generalized abstractions of mathematics and the matter-energy forms of the cosmos should match up so perfectly. Suddenly the generalization of mathematics and the abstraction of Earthly production parted ways. Ideas no longer belonged to a generalized, allegorical medium. The symmetry of grammar and logic failed. The world of the philosophic tradition turned out to be not universal but epochal. We pass from a time of a controlling generality to a time of no controlling generality, no paradigm or episteme. Earthly intelligence tried to sponsor itself with its own underwriting ideas. It worked better than there was any reason to expect for millennia. It gave fragile intelligence a purchase on another kind of Earthly life, but it only took us so far.

The appearance of data as a dimension of the physical site in such mind-blowing quantities transformed the biosphere. Evolution leapt so athletically and discontinuously that neither we nor the bacteria that rapidly evolved to acquire immunity to new antibiotics know what we have done. If life had evolved arduously by natural selection, vertical transmission of data (from parents to off-spring), it suddenly began, as perhaps it did in the beginning, to deploy horizontal and chaotic informational exchange. Speciation and conceptualization crashed together. We now implement ourselves as abstractions that erase their origins and strike out for unknown territory.

This understandably makes people nervous, but there is no backing out. The HumOS has been erased.

The first dimension of information, which is, thus, the fifth dimension of the Earthly knowledge site, is the dimension of short-term memory—the buffers of the many nervous systems, not as a generalization but as countable collections. There are also the data of the past or sixth dimension (history, the photographs in one's data files). The data of the projections of future events is the seventh dimension (extrapolations of all kinds, the models of global warming and the equity markets, whatever intimations of the future, prophecy). The fifth, sixth, and seventh dimensions are relatively unstable and implicated in the uncertain work of knowing and the possibility of being known. They are possibilities that appear and disappear. There are gaps and potential gaps—quantities that may or may not be measurable. And already there begin to be more information dimensions and potential dimensions: the dimensions of virtual worlds and artificial intelligences must also be allotted Earthly spaces of meaning and value. The competing architectural designs for each site in the city or the competing foreign policies of the many governments generate information dimensions. It was said that there are as many spatial dimensions as muscles in the body; there are as many information dimensions as there are ways to know what is knowable. The organized zones appear in a field of possibilities that is likely random, not a single object that can be taken under a single view. Even the distribution of organized zones in the random space may be random. *The evolution of the complex intelligence and creative energy to address this daunting world is the work of investigative poetry.*

The first law of the data site, however, is relatively simple: if complex intelligence is to continue to evolve it must act so there are more possibilities to act next time. This includes both the enrichment of the physical dimensions and the creation of new dimensions. Even people who make many new possibilities, if they use more than they make, are dead ducks. It is a mathematical law.

*   *   *

We will see the day of

RELENTLESS
PURSUIT OF DATA.

Thus far, it seems, we have been more the pursued than the pursuer. All of the science fiction plots are in play. The old forms of knowing are thoroughly disrupted. The arbitrary and the absurd that were used by the Dadaists and surrealists as forms of disruption and revolutionary trouble-making are now tools of control creating noise in the public flow of information (a Trump speech) or decoration (Burning Man, the Olympics). It is necessary to reaffirm the possibility of an Earthly paradise.

The horizon of Investigation is now three years and probably less. One might want to investigate, say, the "social media" or a specific social media site, such as Facebook. The meaning and value of these referents, however, are in flux. The deep meaning "Facebook" changed in 2015 without much notice by its users or anyone else, when an algorithm known as "DeepFace" was deployed on the site. The investigative artist Trevor Paglen writes: "Facebook's 'DeepFace' algorithm produces three-dimensional abstractions of individuals' faces and uses a neural network that achieves over 97 percent accuracy at identifying individuals." As he puts it, you are not so much looking at your picture as your picture is looking at you. This alone might be a change that could bring forth an entirely new culture. One might compare the impact of perspective drawing as a factor in the pervasive cultural change of the Renaissance. New techniques of comparable power now, however, appear regularly. These are epochal days. Everything changes. Change changes. We might pick ourselves up from the tragic mud.

Again Paglen: "There are many [other equally powerful algorithms]: Facebook's "DeepMask" and Google's TensorFlow identify people, places, objects, locations, emotions, gestures, faces, genders, economic statuses, relationships, and much more. In aggregate, AI systems have appropriated human visual culture and transformed it into a massive, flexible training set." (Google Paglen's essay, "Invisible Images (Your Pictures Are Looking at You).")

AI machines, for example, can identify the sexual preferences of people whose pictures appear on dating sites with roughly 90% accuracy (a little less than 90% for women; a little more than 90% for men). They can probably identify political and religious identities and the fans of commercial brands with comparable accuracy or will soon be able to. The amazing fact is that the machines have discovered and applied the crucial features for themselves. Only the machine knows what it is looking for and attempts to translate the data into generalized subject-object language fails. The machine uses protocols that do not require generalized concepts of the kind that underwrite grammar.

I recently heard Paglen speak in connection with his show at Metro Pictures in New York in which he exhibited prints of images by machines for other machines. The first, nervous questions from the audience had to do understandably with how to avoid surveillance. Can you put something over your head? And, of course, to some extent, one can. There may be special kinds of makeup to change one's appearance. One might learn ninja-like moves to make one's way down the street unseen. What you actually look like, however, is mostly irrelevant. The class of people with sacks over their heads also constitutes a viable data set. The color of one's sack may correlate to one's political affiliation or the brand of beer you buy. The machine will, or at least probably can, know. Your credit card bill will reveal where you bought your sacks and how much you paid for them. The investigative artist Hito Steyerl, and sometimes collaborator with Paglen, has a video on Youtube entitled, "How Not to Be Seen: A Fucking Didactic Educational.mov File." It is a Monty Pythonish look at the absurd difficulties of hiding (goggle the title).

Everything one does produces data. Soon almost *everything* about you will be knowable. Even in the most benign of systems, the validity of identity as such is called into question. Who knows if the items on your credit card bill correlate to the imagery of your deep consciousness or your proclivity to subvert governments. This requires a broad re-thinking of *Investigative Poetry*.

Investigative artists, even in regimes where most of the citizens seldom feel the grips of repression, are systematically harassed, intimated, and worse. Laura Poitras, the maker of the film *Citizenfour*, on Edward Snowden, is harassed by Homeland Security every time she returns home to the United States. (Trevor Paglen was the photographer for *Citizenfour.*) Poitras' "Berlin Diary" is a crucial text for a sense of the emotional edge of the new investigative art: "C4 [Snowden] asked me to put a target on his back. To not protect his identity. He also said he would never commit suicide. What kind of fucking world is this when that everyone in my films says this to me." (From *Astro Noise: A Survival Guide for Living Under Total Surveillance*, 2015) What this means, just to be clear, is that the deaths of people involved in anti-surveillance investigations are likely to be reported as suicides.

It is not, however, only the public-private dimension of the data site on which the traditional cultural norms are disrupted. It is clear that computers are more reliable drivers of cars and trucks than people. I was told by a relative, who works in agri-business, that the recent increase in the production of corn per acre has come about not from increased use of fertilizer or the improvement of the genetic structure of corn—these were important in the last century—but because the distance between rows has been reduced from 30 inches to 15 or 20 inches. The effective productivity of an acre may be nearly doubled. This seems an entirely old-fashioned solution, but it belongs entirely to the information age. The old-fashion tractor operators lack the precision of hand-eye coordination and attention to keep tractors between such narrow rows. Tractors on these farms are now computer controlled.

It seems that there are relatively few jobs, from checking out customers at the supermarket to diagnosing and treating illnesses, that will not be better done by machines than by traditional professionals, including the professionals that flip burgers and do janitorial work. The machines may begin to find deep patterns in the databases of disciplinary knowledge. They may be able to reveal larger and more revealing patterns in, say, the nineteenth-century novel than a blood and bones reader (google the research of Franco Moretti. Google may reveal more about Moretti than you bargained for.) We may be relieved of labor, some say we may be relieved of mortality or at least its harshest dimensions.

Investigative artists, however, immediately confront a quandary. On data sites of more or less total surveillance, invisibility seems necessary to individual meaning and value, but it is destructive to the meaning and value of life and art with respect to, and even the possibility of, community. The person of completely secure identity is the loneliest of creatures.

The humans opted for a symmetrical and just world that gave even odds on everything. They flipped a coin and believed the outcome in the sight of the blindfolded lady with the scales would make sense, either or both outcomes would make sense. They were "half in love with easeful death," or a little more than half. It was a tragic world. The Oedipus story explored the deepest mystery of parents and children being different and the same. "The way up and the way down are the same" (Heraclitus). "He that findeth his life shall lose it; and he that loseth his life for my sake shall find it" (Jesus). If it is true, as Carl Jung said, "Only the paradox comes anywhere near to comprehending the fullness of life," there is a still deeper paradox: only the paradox comes anywhere near to comprehending the absurdity and emptiness of life that can only assert itself by consuming itself. *The task of investigative poetry is to burst through the paradox that is implicit in every twenty-four hour news cycle.*

The Single Intelligence is overmatch. There is no place for irony or cynicism. We need syndicates, posses, gangs of poet-investigators, not collaborating on a single project—the Single Project also is overmatched—but coordinating research and creation. The data site is not a single thing. The black boxes of communication exchange inputs and outputs in relation to measures of meaning and value—the creation that everyone can hear and see. The Earth is only prophecy, if it is.

Introduction to *Investigative Poetry*

"This is the Age of Investigation
and every citizen must investigate"

were the opening lines of a poem I read at the New Year's Poetry
Marathon Jan 1, '75 at the St. Mark's Church in NYC. And it actually
WAS a thrilling Age of Investigation after the long years of Johnson,
Nixon, assassinations & secret wars; an era beginning around '74
which compared very well to the Golden Age of Muckrake, when
Ida Tarbell brought down Standard Oil for its predatory evil, as book
publishers, investigative reporters & tv producers all of a sudden
found public support for pieces that looked behind the scenes of
greed, secret violence, the world of the CIA/FBI/Military & corrupt
government, so that the year I wrote *Investigative Poetry* bloomed with
a rising expectation of a better democracy!

We were hoping it to be more peaceful, less hateful, with the
right wing on the ebb, war made more obsolete! and hearing all the
Muses singing the praises of The Age of investigation, as the long and
calamitous war in Vietnam (Laos and Cambodia too), suffused with
napalm and Agent Orange, was headed to a close.

Sy Hersh had recently splashed over the front page of *The New
York Times* the grim history of the CIA's Operation Chaos which
revealed how the Agency had illegally spied on and compiled 10,000
dossiers on various groups and U.S. citizens in violation of the 1947
National Security Act.

And Senator Frank Church began chairing in early 1975 a bi-
partisan Senate Select Committee to Study Governmental Operations
with Respect to Intelligence Activities which conducted eye-opening
hearings on illegal CIA/FBI/NSA intelligence-gathering and covert
operations.

1976 saw a further flowering of the Age of Investigation with the creation of the House Select Committee on Assassinations which conducted reinvestigations of the murders of John F. Kennedy and Martin Luther King, Jr. In 1979, a single Report and twelve volumes of appendices on each assassination were published by the Congress.

So the publication of *Investigative Poetry* by City Lights fit right in with this important Age. I had prepared myself for this, say, ever since the Freedom Rides of 1961. Absorbing the daily surge of headlines, and the long-time influence of mentors such as Allen Ginsberg and Charles Olson provided the intellectual impetus for my manifesto.

I remember purchasing the 1959 Totem Press/Leroi Jones version of Charles Olson's "Projective Verse" from the 8h Street Bookshop soon after it was published. The same year, from the same place, I bought the Auerhahn Press "Maximus from Dogtown— I." Both scorched through my mind, much as "Howl" had done back in 1957.

I began corresponding with Olson in 1962, visited him in Gloucester in 1964, and at the Berkeley Poetry Conference in 1965. And now and then I saw him until just before his passing in early 1970. Ginsberg became a close friend starting in 1964, and he lived just down the street from my Peace Eye Bookstore in the Lower East Side of NY.

When I wrote my book on the Manson group, *The Family*, in 1970 and '71, for the first drafts I tended to write the text in lines breaks and vertical verse-clusters, which I later retyped into regular paragraphs. It was this experience of composing in line-breaks that was instrumental in inspiring me to consider Investigative Poetry.

By the spring of 1975 I was working steadily on Investigative Poetry. I helped organize that spring a series of readings at a bistro on Rock City Road in Woodstock, where Miriam and I and our daughter Deirdre had moved from New York City in '74. During the inspired readings at Rosa's Cantina, I listened and made notes for Investigative Poetry.

I was invited to an International Counterculture Festival in Montreal that spring also and conversations on the concepts of Investigative Poetry I had there with Allen Ginsberg and William Burroughs helped strengthen and turn my notes into a kind of manifesto.

The Counterculture Festival featured William Burroughs, Allen Ginsberg, Claud Pelieu, Mary Beach, Charles Plymell, Denis Vanier, Anne Waldman, John Giorno, and others. This event was titled Rencontre Internationale "de la contreculture," and in addition to a reading, I was invited to give a talk.   That talk was the first version of "Investigative Poetry."

That summer I was invited to read and lecture at the Naropa Institute in Boulder, Colorado, where I spent time with Joanne Kyger, Michael Brownstein, Allen Ginsberg, Phil Whalen, and others. My lecture was the final version of "Investigative Poetry," which I had been polishing and researching, using the Woodstock Library during many afternoons.

Joanne Kyger was on hand for my lecture, and soon urged Lawrence Ferlinghetti and City Lights Books to publish it. To my lasting gratitude Ferlinghetti had it well-designed and printed it in late 1976.

Thanks, Lawrence
Thanks, Joanne
Thanks, Don Byrd, for urging this republication
Thanks, Michael Boughn, for typing and overseeing it
Thanks to the Age of Investigation
                              in full-swell during the mid-late 1970s!

And thanks also to George Butterick, who was in charge of the Charles Olson Archive at the Wilbur Cross Library at the University of Connecticut during those years, and who wrote me in early December 1976, after reading the newly published *Investigative Poetry:*

"Dear Ed,

Let me tell you your *Investigative Poetry* is one of the most important documents, texts, textbooks, and manifestos or manifestations to come into my hands since—I guess it's the most important thing for me since "Projective Verse" itself. That's a big claim, I know, but I can't see any other way around it and no other contender intervenes in my mind. The language is so accessible and such a clarion into the cold morning air, like reveille. I tell all the students who come to me to acquire it....

The only thing that has me puzzled is why you left out what for me is the obvious guiding and controlling quotation for all of Olson (from "A Bibliography on America"):

        Best thing to do is *to dig one thing or place or man* until you yourself know more about
        that than is possible to any other man. It doesn't matter whether it's Barbed Wire
        or Pemmican or Paterson or Iowa. But *exhaust* it. Saturate it. Beat it.
                    And then U
KNOW everything else
        very fast: one saturation job (it might take 14 years).
        And you're in, forever

It is the one principle that has guided me all the while. Poor Charles didn't know it would be turned upon himself! although he was using himself and Melville as the example of the "14 years."

George Butterick"

Thank you, George Butterick, and all hail the Age of Investigation!.

—Ed Sanders

INVESTIGATIVE POETRY

Investigative Poetry: that poetry
should again assume responsibility
for the description of history

SECTIONS

1. The content of history will be poetry
2. Techniques of investigative poetry
3. Presenting data on the page —the page is the history
4. Some observations on the public performances of investigative poets

Lecture Prepared
For the Visiting Spontaneous
Poetics Academy.
The Naropa Institute
Boulder, Colorado
July 8, 1975 —and revised
in the
fall of 1975 and winter of '76

Ed Sanders

A note of thanks to Rick Fields and Larry Mermelstein of the Naropa Institute; to Allen Ginsberg who sets for all time the example that rebel poets not allow themselves to be driven into isolation; to ace private investigator Larry Larsen for much quiet counseling re: concepts of data-forage; to Thorpe Menn who graciously allowed the use of his desk at the *Kansas City Star* for preliminary typing; and. to the Woodstock Library for its fine collection of Coleridge, Shelley and other bards.

And to the memory of Charles Olson
Read his books.

move over Herodotus
move over Thuc'
move over Arthur Schlesinger
move over logographers and chroniclers
and compulsive investigators

for the poets
are marching again
upon the hills
of history

The Content of History Will be Poetry

———————————————

———————————————

> There is no end
> to *Gnosis:*
>
> The hunger
> for *DATA*

A.

The Goal: an era of investigative poesy wherein one can be controversial, radical, and not have the civilization rise up to smite down the bard. To establish and to maintain it. POETS MAY REMAIN IN THE RADIX, UNCOMPROMISING, REVOLUTIONARY, SEDITIOUS, ABSOLUTE.

POET as Investigator
Interpreter of Sky Froth
Researcher of the Abyss
Human Universer
Prophet
Prophet without death
as a consequence.

My statement is this: that poetry, to go forward, in my view, has to begin a voyage into the description of *historical reality*.

Last winter I was examining the text, and the history of the composition, of Hart Crane's *The Bridge*, and I was struck by the historical scholarship the poet had undertaken in the five or so years he labored in its composition. Crane consulted numerous books on American history, building a ziggurat of scholarship with which, as the poet intended, *The Bridge* might confront the dry neo-Pindarian puritan sonorities of the *Wasteland*, which much of *The Bridge* was intended to confront.

In addition, for 15 years I had followed the work and career of Charles Olson, particularly the *Maximus* Poems, and the poems contained in that Grove Press book, *The Distance*, and was always amazed how Charles, with his enormous intellect and energy, was able, by consulting old city files— that is, books and documents relating to a formerly obscure New England fishing settlement, Gloucester, Massachusetts—to transform these researches into high-order poetry, using his principles of *composition by field* as enumerated in his projective verse manifesto, the result being poetry as history, or history-poesy, or Clio come down to Gloucester in a breeze of High Energy Verse Grids, or Data Clusters, a form of poetic presentation I will discuss in greater detail later.

And then there is the matter of *Howl*. When *Howl* was published in the '50s, it was accepted for what it was, a religious document of great beauty and awesome threnodic power, and a work, we were rightly certain, destined to change American history. Its IMPLICATIONS were historical. As years went by, and the analysis of the poem continued, I time-tracked the poem's implications as they oozed into the historical lifestyle plexus. So doing, I came to greater and greater awareness of the poet's investigative techniques.

That is, *Howl*, with its wonderful fresh combinations of ancient Greek metres combined with long held-breath lines lasting, in some cases, 5 to 10 seconds, is a work of American history. I remember this spring reading a book called *The Beat Book,* published by Arthur and Glee Knight; particularly the interview with Carl Solomon, who relates in that great Solomonian mode, how Ginsberg was always, in the classic gum-shoe, or muse-sandal, manner, asking oodles of questions of his friends, clarifying anecdotes, keeping files on all his friends, many of which anecdotes and data-files turning up later on in *Howl*. In fact, from an examination of the anecdotes in Howl, we may devolve one of the first rules of Investigative Poetry: Do not hesitate to open up a case file on a friend.

A good example is the famous Mallarmé potato salad toss, immortalized by the bard on page 15 of the City Lights edition of *Howl and other Poems:*

> who threw potato salad at CCNY lecturers on Dadadism and
>> subsequently presented themselves on the granite steps of
>> the madhouse with shaven heads and harlequin speech of
>> suicide, demanding instant lobotomy ...

In the interview in *The Beat Book,* Solomon confirms the historicity of such a 'tato-toss, but corrects the poetic license of the poem by pointing out that the salad hurling, performed by Solomon and several friends, rather than occurring during a lecture on dadaism, occurred in the course of a lecture on Mallarmé given by Wallace Markfield.

B. Investigative Eleutherarchs

Lawyers have a term: "to make law." You "make law" when you're involved in a case or an appeal which, as in Supreme Court decisions which have expanded the scope of personal freedom, opens up new human avenues.

You make law.

Bards, in a similar way, "make reality," or, really, they "make freedom" or they create new modes of what we might term Eleutherarchy, or the dance of freedom.

C. The Legacy of Ezra Pound

Purest Distillations from the Data-Midden: the essence of Investigative Poetry: Lines of lyric beauty descend from the data clusters.

The Cantos of Ezra Pound first gave us melodic blizzards of data-fragments. History as slime-sift for morality; Olson grew out of that Poundian concern. I don't personally believe an Investigative Poet has to research *The Cantos* for clues to the future. More of the mode of futurity might be learned by studying Pound's *Confucian Odes,* certainly some of the most beautiful and varied melodies anyone has written. On the other hand, who can deny the didactically overpowering drill-job that Canto 45, or 81, performed upon our unsuspecting brows. I remember hitchhiking around the country in the late '50s, the only books in my pack, besides *Buddhist Texts through the Ages,* being *Howl,* D. Thomas's *Collected Poems,* Kant's *Prolegomenon to Any Future Metaphysics,* and *The Cantos.* And it was *The Cantos* that trapped one forever in its warp.

Pound gave us shaped texts: some of his pages, such as 81, and, say 75 (Out of Phlegethon!), and many to be found even by a quick spiffle through the pages: THESE PAGES, IN CONSIDERATION OF THEIR SHAPE AND ARRANGEMENTS OF DATA-GRIDS, ARE OF BEAUTY. That is, Pound helped verse escape the dungeon of the column inch.

And Pound was a skilled collagist: and the lesson is this: that an Investigative Poet of any worth at all will have to become as skilled a collagist as the early Braque.

The poetry of *The Cantos* would emerge, as it were, from a plexus of memories, quote-torrents from the Greek, Latin, Italian, Chinese, French, Arabic, Egyptian, *et al.,* from quick historical vignettes, even, like, newspaper headlines, whereupon, on a sudden, flash! the essence appears; an exquisite line begins and a cadence of purest verse thrills the-eye-brain.

Thus Olson, thus Ginsberg, thus Investigative Poetry. The fault of Pound's epic, in my opinion, is that it races too near the course of Achilles, of war lords, of patriarchal death-breaths. And it speaks, in my opinion, too strongly in favor of a society run by austere whip-freaks and fascists, and it condones Hitlerism and anti-Semitism.

On the other hand, Pound's insight into the money-hallucinated-out-of-nothing nature of the banking system, where sleazisms like David Rockefeller can create money by whim, has been an inspiration to many a poor poet trying to scrounge up even a quarter to buy an egg-cream at Gem Spa's.

And the important lesson we can learn from Pound, in the matter of writing investigative poetry, or history-poetry, is never to allow hatred of a data-target, or the heat of a case, to arouse one, or to wire one up, to the point of insanity, or violence, or to the condoning of racism, or killing. Treason against gentleness.

D.

It is therefore my belief that virtually every major poet's work in France and America for the past 100 years has prepared the civilization for the rebirth of history poesy. The *Wasteland, The Bridge, The Cantos,* W. C. Williams' *Paterson, The Maximus Poems,* Ginsberg's *Ankor Wat, Howl* and *Wichita Vortex Sutra,* the work of Snyder, in, say, *Turtle Island,* and Jerome Rothenberg in *Poland 1931,* all betoken an era of investigative poesy, a form of historical writing—this is as potentially dangerous to the poet as a minefield or those small foot-snuffing blow-up devices the defense dept. used in Vietnam; but it is a danger thrillsomely magnetic to a bard wandering through the electromagnetic aeon.

History-poesy, or investigative poetry, can thrive in our era because of the implications of a certain poetic insight, that is, in the implications of the line, "Now is the time for prophecy without death as a consequence," from "Death to Van Gogh's Ear," a Ginsberg poem from 1958.

Investigative poesy is freed from capitalism, churchism, and other totalitarianisms; free from racisms, free from allegiance to napalm-dropping military police states—a poetry adequate to discharge from its verse-grids the undefiled high energy purely-distilled verse-frags, using *every* bardic skill and meter and method of the last 5 or 6 generations, in order to describe *every* aspect (no more secret governments!) of the historical present, while aiding the future, even placing bard-babble once again into a role as shaper of the future.

For this is the era of the description of *the All*; the age wherein a Socrates would have told the judges to take a walk down vomit alley, and could have lived as an active vehement leader of the Diogenes Liberation Squadron of Strolling Troubadours and Muckrakers, till the microbes 'whelmed him. The era of police-statists punishing citizens for secret proclivities is over. Blackmail, in other words, is going to go bye-bye. One will not in any way have to assure one's readers (to quote, is it Martial, or Catullus?) that "*pagina lasciva, vita proba*" but rather it is now most definitely the age of "*pagina pagina lasciva, vita lascivior.*" And we are here speaking of uncompunctious conjugation, not of richies cutting up cattle from silent helicopters, or of bankers whipping each other on yachts.

Thrills course upward from the typewriter keys as my fingers type the words that say that poets are free from the nets of any *particular* verse-form or verse-mind. Keats would have grown old in such a freedom. The days of bards chanting dactylic hexameters while strumming the phormingx, or lyre, trying to please some drooly-lipped warlord are over, o triumphant beatnik spores! It's over! And the days of bards trying to please some CIA-worshipping cold war tough-liberal professor are done! done! done!

But the way of Historical Poesy, as I said earlier, is mined with danger, especially to those bards who would seek to drag the corpses of J.P. Morgan's neo-confederates through the amphetamine piranha tank.
For let us not forget for one microsecond that the government throughout history has tried to supress, stomp down, hinder, or buy off dissident or left-wing poets.[1]

One has only to recall that Coleridge and Wordsworth one day were lounging by the sea shore, while nearby sat an English police agent on snitch patrol prepared to rush to headquarters to quill a report about the conversation.[2]

Or one can read that remarkable book, *William Blake and the Age of Revolution* by J. Bronowski, which Harper & Row printed in 1965, to see how reactionary English creeps, with their threats of jail, or worse, for accurately depicting the nature of the early parts of the French Revolution, —how these reactionary creeps caused, in a significant way, poets like William Blake, who after all was a friend of Thomas Paine, to back away from historical poetry, and to retreat, if that is the word, into a poetry of symbols, where people like King George and William Pitt and others were known by code names such as Palamabron and Rintrah.[3]

Nor let us forget that the federal government tried to seize the first printing of *Howl and Other Poems* (it was printed abroad by City Lights) as it was coming into San Francisco bay.

Nor shall we forget the repressive corona of puke-vectors that I believe drove Shelley —censored, hounded by police statists, fearful of arrest— to take upon himself a self-destruction (rest in peace, o d.a. levy) and to set sail into a mad air; nor forget ever the corona of puke-vectors that sent the empty carriages of the rich shuttling along behind the cortege bearing the body of Byron.[4]

Nor shall we forget the fate of Ovid, who because that calmed-down murderer, Augustus, didn't like his book and the implications of his book *Ars Amatoria,* was sent away from the literary scene to die in exile.[5]

Nor shall we forget that Dostoevsky was standing ready to die in front of the firing squad when the reprieve arrived enabling him later on to "objectify" his stance into that of a jealous rightwing nut.[6]

Nor shall we forget how the Chilean poet-singer Victor Jara was leading a group of singers while imprisoned in the soccer stadium following the 1973 CIA-coup in Chile, and the killers chopped off his fingers to silence his guitar, and still he lead the singing—till they killed him, another bard butchered because of the U.S. secret police.

Nor shall we forget how the Czar's secret police hounded Alexander Pushkin with a nightmare of surveillance and exile. In fact, a brief look at certain aspects of Pushkin's life is here appropriate, in order to gauge some of the pressures that can force a poet "to become more objective," or, as the English professor who writes for a CIA-funded magazine might giggle, "to come to terms with the harsh facts of life." Or to escape into the forgetful symbols.

FOOTNOTES: Section I

1. *The Secret Police Sell-out Rule*: time after time as we read the biographies of writers~ our hearts are broken as we monitor a hideous drift, passing, say, the 33rd year, to the cautious right. Sometimes I think that the secret police of the world developed a procedure at least 300 years ago to deal with the potential of the brilliant young to create quick change. And the Secret Police Sell-out Rule would go something like this: "If you can stomp them and punish them enough in their youth and middle age, then they'll calm down, the punks, and silently assent to the Corrupting It." Energy bio-dwindle also adds to the sell-out rule. And, if I go to prison, what will happen to my 15,000 books?

2. Someone should write well the story of Citizen Threlwell. If we all do not have the free chance to enact our own Threlwellian maneuvers, then we are still slaves. The point is that a visit by Threlwell was enough to cause you (Wordsworth) to lose your house and for the fuzz to slap a surveillance on you.

3. We are not here saying that Blake's *The French Revolution* is the world's greatest poem. And obviously Rintrah is a much more groovy name than Henry Kissinger (one way to deal with baleful names such as Kissinger's, in poems would be, as the language gets more "glyphic" again, to conceive of a cacoglyph —a drawing or symbol (cacoglyph being the opposite of the sacred-or hieroglyph) depicting, say, Kissinger. But we must, on the other hand, be wary of polishing such specks of evil till they become our shiniest art, if you can scan my zone.

John Clarke, certainly one of the finest scholars of Blake, responded to the manuscript of *Investigative Poetry* with a poem, which speaks right to the essence of the Blake problem:

AS TO THE DISSIMULATION

It is true certainly Blake suffered from
Nervous Fear & because of it retreated into
a poetry of symbols, but, ironically, this
retreat was truer to his Good Angel than
had he quickly & easily- like Oedipus solved,
being a Mental Prince, the ease of history
under investigation, for, lo & behold, he found
something deeper behind, going on, States
which only Individuals were in, not fused with
Eternally, but retrievable, a true cosmological
narrative to be written as distinct from its
Generated denominations, whose accomplishment
is only what allows us today to be political,
his system gave us the tools of our profession.

Sept 17, 1975

Yes. And Blake's stance is **Absolute Integrity,** without which Investigative
Poetry is immoral gibberish —-and his drive toward the hieratic poem-
glyph is ever our investigative grail.

And I have no quarrel with Blake's vision of a whole system of Self—a
Self that paints, designs and sings the limitations of God or Godot or
Gododd. What I quarrel with is the withdrawal from the polis—and into
the polis thus neglected *will* march totalitarian apostles: nixon, hitler, stalin,
haldeman, helms—abetted by the kings and queens of satan (the lovers of
violence).

> About 1789
> William Blake moved to small house
> on south side of Thames
>
> got cooking there
> on Prophetic Books

decided through visits and advice of the
received ghost of his brother Robert

to design in reverse relief on etched
copper plates, both poem and design—

and then to adorn the printed-
poem with individual paintings

thank you, o ghost.

    Hand-held press
    Hand-etched copper plates
    Hand-pigmented poem-glyphs
    The hand! The hand!

And as he fashioned and painted more and more of his books

    He moved
    Toward
    Soul-Scroll.

And Blake's techniques in preparing and producing say, *The Songs of Innocence and Experience,* the move toward poem-glyph, should ever be an archetype for the Investigative Poet. Print it yrself, adorn it yrself, send it out yrself, and make it sacred.

[4.] Shelley and government spy-scum: "At last he gave up, sent forward a box filled with his books, which was inspected by the government and reported as seditious, and on April 4 left Ireland (1812). He settled ten days later at Nantgwilt, near Cwm Elan, the seat of his cousins, the Groves, and there remained until June. In this period he appears to have met Peacock, through whom he was probably introduced to his London Publisher, Hookham. In June he again migrated to Plymouth in Devon.

Here he wrote his 'Letter to Lord Ellenborough,' defending Eaton, who had been sentenced for publishing Paine's *Age of Reason* in a periodical. He amused himself by putting copies of the *Declaration of Rights*, (Shelley's revolutionary pamphlet from French sources) and a new satirical poem, "The Devil's Walk," in bottles and fire balloons, and setting them adrift by sea and air; but a more mundane attempt to circulate the *Declaration of Rights* resulted unfortunately for his servant (I guess we have to forgive Shelley for having servants), who had become attached to him and followed him from Ireland, and was punished by a fine of 200 pounds or eight month's imprisonment for posting it on the walls of Barnstable. Shelley could not pay the fine, but he provided fifteen shillings a week to make the prisoner's confinement more comfortable. *The government now put Shelley under surveillance, and he was watched by Leeson, a spy* . . . and it is known that Shelley was dogged by Leeson, whom he feared long afterwards."

> from the biographical sketch in
> *Complete Poetical Works of*
> *Percy Bysshe Shelley*
> Cambridge Edition, 1901

> There is nothing like having a hateful person, paid by a
> government agency, company or private party, enter your life
> spewing nodules of mix-up, dissension, hate, violence, fear.
> (take a quick check into the specifics for instance, of the FBI
> cointelpro fear-and-death ruinations.)

5. Every time I get out my 11th edition of the *Encyclopaedia Britannica* (vol. 20, ODE to PAY), I suffer the frothing anger-electrics reading about the injustices suffered by Ovid, driven to the Black Sea by a punk turkey tyrant snuffer. And it could well happen again—the androids with book-burning lasers to knock at a poet's door with a computerized printout of the plot of her latest poem.

6. One can understand how Dostoevsky drifted to the right, being a heavy Russian nationalist at heart—but o lord how could he have ever accepted inside himself, first that he deserved a sentence of death, or deserved a commutation that gave him 5 hideous years in the slams, and for what? For *conspiring to print* copies of Belinsky's revolutionary letter of response to the late life god-grovels of Gogol.

Alexandr Pushkin

d.o.b. 5-26-1799
d. 1-29-1837
shot in stomach

friends
with pre-Decembrists
secret societies, but never trusted with

plot-plans.   They never trust poets.

belonged to Green Lamp which may have
been a branch of the Union of Welfare, freethinking
orgiasts and partisans of Liberty.

Pushkin's cry of "Tremble, o tyrants of the world
And you ... o fallen slaves, arise!"
(Ode to Freedom, 1817

may not have been so loudly heard in the casinos of Petrograd but it is said
that the revolutionary poems of his youth were so sung in the mind that the
soldiers in the barracks knew them by heart

—9 of 10, it is said, of the young in Russia then received their
revolutionary input from Pushkin.

His political poems, like the secret Russian tracts of today, were passed
from hand to hand in manuscript.

The fuzz were hip to the trip, and harassed Pushkin. In 1820, he nearly was
bricked into prison, so chose a period of exile in the south.

During these years of police surveillance, Pushkin gradually began to soften under the pressure, becoming "more objective"—that is, secreting his revolutionary politics in narrative.

6 years of police harassment, til Sept of 1826, the new Czar, Nicolas I, summoned him to Moscow, and announced that he, the Czar, henceforth would be the poet's "censor." And although the poet's formal exile was over, the chief of the Russian Secret Police kept him under the shackles of surveillance. Pushkin had to submit all his writings to the Czar for approval.

In March of 1826, he was to write in a letter, "I do not intend foolishly to oppose the generally accepted order." (As, and probably under similar fearful pressure, William Blake in 1791 had decided not to print *The French Revolution*.)

Three years
Pushkin in Moscow and Petrograd, a dissipated period of surveillance, drinking, gambling, fucking—wrote very little—a right-winger's vision of paradise for a poet.
1927/8/9

And in the 1830's Pushkin studied in the Russian State Archives going back to the texts and documents.

Pressure
        force the poets
                pressure
                    to weaken
                        pressure
                            the force

        of their beliefs.

    Never Again.

E.

At the great religious
festivals of antiquity
the poets sang/chanted
for prizes—

and in the era of the Investigative Poet
the Diogenes Troubadour Data Squads
will chew their way into the
gory dressing room of Richard Helms

But what is the prize?
The prize is for the poets
to assume their rightful
positions as chroniclers
of the Time Track,
of the historical moment
whether century, aeon, hour
or microsecond

As Olson said: "I would be an historian as Herodotus Was, looking for
oneself for the evidence of what is said."

But what is the prize?
the prize is for Diogenes Eleutherarchs
waving the banner of
enforced economic equality
to weaken, to lessen,
and to bring down into the vale of Ha Ha Hee
the North American CIA Police State,

and for poets
never again
to internalize groveless.

SECTION 2

Techniques of Investigative Poetry

A. Projective Verse

Charles Olson's elucidation in his essay manifesto "Projective Verse" of the principle of COMPOSITION BY FIELD has opened up the way for poets to get back into such historical description in an important way.

> The verse of the investigative poet of
> genius will discharge data as if scanning
> eye-brains were passing across a high-energy grid,
> the vectors of verse-froth leaping up from
> the verse-grids at every point. High Energy
> Verse History Grids!

"A poem is energy transferred from where the poet got it, by way of the poem itself to, all the way over to, the reader."

and

"Then the poem must, at all points, be a high energy-construct and, at all points, an energy-discharge."

Olson, "Projective Verse"

and

"We now enter ... the large area of the whole poem, into the FIELD ... where all the syllables and all the lines must be managed in their relation to each other."

and

"the HEAD, by way of the EAR, to the SYLLABLE
the HEART, by way of the BREATH, to the LINE"

I can't tell *you* how excited I am, personally, about the concept of history-
verse, of high energy data grids—

> "ONE PERCEPTION MUST IMMEDIATELY
> AND DIRECTLY LEAD TO A FURTHER
> PERCEPTION"
> > Olson, quoting Edward Dahlberg
> > again from "Projective Verse"

> The Illumination-sparks flood into
> the mind all along
> > and at every point
> > of the Data Grid!

"It is a matter, finally of OBJECTS," Olson says,

"of OBJECTS, what they are, what they are inside
a poem, how they got there, and, once there,
how they are to be used."

B. Concerning
The Opening of case files

Files age
Files wax rusty
The data corrodes
by the tendency of
poets to escape into
the symbols.

And this: that ne'er too 'plete nor pullulated w/plies are your cases. Nor is it ever done:

> One's file, you know, is never quite complete; a case is never really closed, even after a century, when all the participants are dead," the British intelligence officer who narrates Graham Greene's *The Third Man* tells us, eyeballing our fast corroding files with a baleful glance that seems to say: even in the midst of an investigation, keep it unchaotic, neat, orderly, perfectly proportioned and terminal. Neat Grids shape the future.

And as for the symbols:

we have already mentioned Blake's work on the French Revolution which he decided not to print; and the later work of Pushkin; how all this talk how poets calm down, how they "come to terms with it," how they become "more objective" is bunk from a punk; and is, in my opinion, a result of repression from governments, and the repression is due, in great part, to the efforts of secret domestic intelligence police. This is true from ancient Egypt, to modern America, France, The Soviet Union; you name the country. Hitler, after World I, led domestic intelligence assassination operations against leftists and intellectuals. Nixon and Haldeman and the FBI-CIA-Surrealistic-Complex were headed the same direction. Case files pulled down the death's-head fluttering above the White House.

Dostoevsky wrote *The Possessed* because of his revulsion at Nechayev, a far left slasher who had set up a network of terror cells each unaware of the other, like bricks in a pyramid, to perform terrorist chop-up capers. He netted some marks for the scam, except the system of 5-unit cells seems to have been mostly in his mind. Dostoevsky overdubbed his own story, including some of his own personal problems, atop the facts of the case, and changed the names. Maybe, however, he should have raced after a few data-targets in the Russian abyss—like visiting Nechayev a few times in Peter and Paul fortress, where Nechayev was being held for the murder of a hesitant cell member. The history of later terrorism might have been changed by it.

Eleutherarchy has taken to the airwaves
since the days of Dostoevsky, however, and
the freedom is there

Therefore, NEVER HESITATE TO OPEN
        UP A CASE FILE

        EVEN UPON THE BLOODIEST OF BEASTS OR PLOTS

C. <u>We will see the day of</u>

        RELENTLESS
        PURSUIT OF DATA!

        Interrogate the Abyss!

To go after an item of time,

        (as Olson says: p. 134 of
        The Human Universe and Other Essays,

        the essence is to
        "KNOW THE NEW FACTS EARLY.")

(After all, wasn't one of the shrieks of our generation to suck eternity from
The NOW, to hear in Sonny Rollins' saxophone, to hear in Snyder and
Burroughs, to hear in meditation and mountain caves, the beauty of the
present, of instant gratification, of word-wheel and world-wheel.)

Therefore how in tune with our era it is
to open up a case file on an item of current time,

and, to quote Olson, this time
to say that history is "Whatever happens,
and if it is significant enough to be recorded
the amount of time of the event can be *minute.*"

minute!!!!!

To surround an item of time
with thick vector-clusters of
Gnosis,

to weave a corona
of perception through verse
and through those *high
energy verse grids* which
we mentioned earlier.

D.   Investigative Glyphs

Draw a graph or glyph
of your investigation target

surround the glyph
with gnosis-vectors

pointing to the target

and never surrender!

robot targeting
                    knocked away
                                    get on feet
                                                prepare new question lists

                    approach the target
                    again again again

                    The Item of Time
                    forever caught & exposed
                    & explicated

                    in the thews & thongs &
                    melodies of bard-babble.

                    ahhh sweet nets
                    of bard-babble.

E. Concerning Shyness
and Investigative Poetry

                                data
                            data cluster
                    data cluster data cluster data cluster
        data cluster   DATA CLUSTER   data cluster
        data cluster   (The Big D)   data cluster
        data cluster   data cluster
        data cluster   DATA CLUSTER   data cluster
                    data cluster data cluster data cluster
                            data cluster
                                data

To *unpeel* the data clusters (to get to the Big D) as well as to fashion them
into skeins of syllables and vowel-melodies and poesy.

People with shyness problems
who want to
get into investigations
have a great obstacle
to overcome.

Do not be afraid
to one-on-one
your Data Target
in the Abyss.

And do not hesitate
to open up a case file
on anything or anybody!

When in doubt,
interrogate, rhapsodize a weave,
or q-quilt or question quilt,
type up a question list.

"If a man or woman does not live
in the thought that he or she
is a history, he or she
is not capable of
himself or herself

saith Olson
p. 28, of *The
Special View of History*

F. The Catalogue of Ships Problem

One of the greatest practical problems, both for the poet and for the reader, in Investigative Poesy, is data-midden boredom —a problem which might be called "The Catalogue of Ships Problem." That is, the boredom a reader often encounters when wading through book two of the *Iliad*, which cloy-gluts even the most eager minds with an endless dactylic dah-da-da dah-da-da parade of description, of the names of the captains & chieftains & gore-goons, and the number of ships in their commands, of the Achaean military array that sailed upon Troy.

As of the catalogue of ships problem, Allen G. suggested (April 1975, Gobelet Rest. in Montreal) that at the "top and bottom of each page, sort of a ticker tape to run to tell what significant info is in the sandwiched page."

The art of the excellent footnote is ever to be practiced. The long poems of Shelley, and particularly Byron, hold excellent models of the brilliant footnote. A foot note is a satellite data-cluster in whose gnarls the poet can skip centuries literally to utter satellite comments upon current events, upon her/his love life, upon any refreshing spark that thrills the eye.

Other aspects of the catalogue of ships problem will be discussed in Section III (the poem on the page), and Section IV (some notes on the public performance of Investigative Poets.)

G. Flashlights to Find the Flashlights

Ezra Pound said, in effect, that historians should leave well-defined gaps in the text or in the presentation equal to the circumstances concerning which they have no knowledge:

that is, their AREAS OF DARKNESS.
When you open a file, the first concern is to define
the AREA OF DARKNESS—-

and to bring the Darkness
the "hard Sophoclean light."

FILES

a) alphabetical —human
b) alphabetical —subject narratives
c) chrono-ooze files, that is, chronological Time Trackings—
>   —relentlessly to pack polished data-gnarls all along the points of a Time Track where the data fits. Chrono-ooze files, when brilliantly engendered, are the most difficult, since it is in time-tracking that epic Investigative Poesy is born.

d) subject-clusters
>   —files relating to a subject that are clustered in vertical shafts upon the same locality, or time period, or upon the same theme.

Subject clusters drive vertical pylons or data-posts here and there in the same time and in the same culture.

(e) system of easily retrievable photos, tape recordings, videotapes, microfilm, etc. Always write the date, the place, the time, and a written description of the contents of material on tapes, photos, etc. You can guess the time that will save you later on. An obscure note, noted only because a crazed-with-data discipline caused you to write everything down, many times will assume great importance six months, or a year even, from the time of its jotting.

(f) index cross-file, if you have the time.
>   —a way out of the enormous tedium of cross index filing, is CONSTANTLY TO REVIEW every single one of your files on the cases at hand,

so that each file has a list of questions to be asked (if you have a typed list of questions ready 24 hours a day, should a data-source be encountered, say, at 3 A.M. at a party, then even if your mind is dialed out into a mode of wastage, the questions are there on the page in grey formality) regarding each file's AREA OF DARKNESS.

(g) a single file of questions, culled from all your files, for the entire case. This is useful when encountering unexpected information sources. Often when you interview someone on one matter, they will have data on other matters as well—-so if you have a huge, organized list of questions on your whole study, then . . .

(h) Cynicism analysis.   This is useful when encountering fresh or shocking or incongruous information. Compare the new information with known data, then make a point by point list to *specify* exactly where the data is at variance with what you know or believe to be correct—-then go back to the original texts, to the tapes, to the living sources, for elucidation. It also helps to have a few trusted highly cynical friends upon whose minds you can unleash your goat-pen of files and your gnarls of investigation, in order to receive the Cynicism Spew, which often may involve guffaws, sneers, snorts of derision, anger, putdowns, abuse, in addition to gentle and very useful location of bullshit nodules within your research.

H. Morality Lists, Event Grids, & Garbage Grids — exhaustive lists w/which to focus in on a person or event.

In Gilbert Sorrentino's novel, *The Imaginative Qualities of Actual Things* (Pantheon 1971), we encounter a literary phenomenon which I have called The Sorrentino Morality List, that is, the numbered descriptive lists he places within the narrative to describe the character or proclivities of a subject. The Morality Lists explain in often humorous detail a person's tendencies, without the encumbrances of paragraphing and excess pronouncing and connectives. In other words a Morality List is facets and facts positioned on a naked fork of numbers. For examples, see pages 15, 16, 194, 195 of *The Imaginative Qualities of Actual Things.* In a recent conversation, Sorrentino told us that in his just-completed book, there is a list some 400 numbered units long. A Morality List does not have to be ha ha handpuppets. It can be in an extremely serious mode, or it can be a mix of serio-ha ha, tragi-ha ha, metaphysical ha ha, and even Wm Blake Laughing Song ha ha.

In addition to Morality Lists, you could present a numbered list relative to a specific event: an event grid—-thus escaping the problem of newspaper reportage, i.e., one grape in a paragraph of sawdust (of ands, ofs, fors, and repetitives). An event Grid can drape or adorn a moment of time with an exhaustive series of numbered clusters.

As of coming to terms with Character. That is, a Morality List, say of Henry Kissinger, who apparently belches and is seized with violence spasms in the planning of bombings such as against Cambodia; such a Morality List, by the depiction of evilness spasms, would turn into a Garbage Grid.

> Olson said, "I wd be an historian as Herodotus was."

> Which is fine indeed, since Herodotus set the parameters of personal investigation.

One has, however, ever to be reminded that a historian, especially a brilliant one, has to be wary of his or her own garbage grids. The Scythians, and Scythian civilization—οι σκυθοι—are forever garbaged by the way Herodotus treated them in his history—so that when museums have exhibitions of Scythian art and artifacts, the catalogue has to encounter and to hurl back a little garbage upon Herodotus himself. Ahh how history loves to garbage the garbagers.

One useful method, if you find yourself preparing garbage grids, and you want to MAINTAIN ACCURACY, is to prepare some garbage grids on YOURSELF

> self-garbage
> see how you like
> it—

> Garbage Grid
> on Self,

that in the end that justice pulse along your grids of others.

I.   The Ha Ha Ha Problem

To be Stubborn in your pursuit of truth
even if it is as if
everyone has ha ha's for your work (whether derision
ha ha's or the ha ha hee of Blake's Laughing Song).

Concerning Derision:

(at a new generation of Investigative Poets)

People might laugh.
And laugh they will.
And laugh they should.
But their laughter may well
be the laughter
of
> The Rasp/Hasp/Asp

(On the other hand we should never forget
how valuable a tool in the tides of social transformation
the subtle use of the Ha Ha He of William
Blake's Laughing Song *IS*:

as of: the mystery of joy in adversity—

    "Come live & be merry and Join with me,
    To sing the sweet chorus of Ha, Ha He.")

J.   <u>Did not Wm Blake urge poets
  to practice practice practice?</u>

Billions of notebooks
Practice writing up
your interview notes
into spontaneous
verse-grids.

Type up
correlative
verse-grids
after the interview.

Even as, say, you talk
to someone over the phone,
as you talk, write down
the data into verse-grids:
TRANSLATE it into
breath-units & poem-lines
With practice, you
can do it automatically.

Write everything down:
You will feel, as a case expands,
filing cabinet into filing cabinet,
like a N.Y. subway shopping bag
roamer

When practicing
writing up Morality Lists or data-grids
you will feel
the lines break—
you will automatically break
your data torrent on
the lines.

In order to depict action in its own time; that is, to capture a real, even a dangerous or frenzied event, in a lattice of poem-lines "as it occurs" is a skill not immediately available.

There is something paralyzing about a powerful event, and observers can often come away with a notepad full of nothing—- or full of inapplicable gibberish.

So it is useful to practice time-tracking. William Burroughs published an essay on this subject in the mid-60's in the *London Sunday Times*> I believe.

The suggestion was, say, to board a bus, and to dial the mind to Total Data, or Total Enternoia, and to widen the peripheral vision, like a basketball player about to make a back-pass. Then to sit: watch for connections; note down the layout; describe the movements of the face muscles of those in your sight—noting the *differences*. Observe what people are reading. Take a 15 minute trip, write a 20 page report.

Try the Total Data mind-dial technique at murder trials, in street riots, at your parents' bridge club, at the intermissions of poetry readings, during bliss, during anger, etc.

In facing hostile data-sources, the main rule is persistent politeness. A persistent politeness that refuses to wax deflected in any way from the data-target.

So many investigative reporters live in alcoholic upper-downer unmeditative total chaos, bouncing from bad news to bad news (which is one of the reasons——in order to strike a balance of peace—to open up "friendship files," that is, files on benevolent and thrilling subjects, such as your best friend), that their view of the universe is correspondingly dour and chaotic.

And just as in certain detective stories, the detective· sometimes sits in one spot, perhaps for hours, sifting the data of a case at great meditative length upon their mind-screen, looking for a "solution" to the case, or for patterns to form in the data-gnarls, so too, in my opinion, investigative poets will want to set up a system of personal meditation, both to keep down the tides of investigative paranoia, and to paint mental data-wheels, and to bring the Chaos to quietude.

Such meditation would certainly help to center the poet, who, say just last night had gotten roughed up trying to walk past Frank Sinatra's body-guards in Las Vegas to try to ask him a few questions about his buddy Sam Giancana and CIA assassination squads.

When facing or working gingerly around a hostile data-source, always remember to let a close friend, or even the police, know where you are going, and when you will be finished, and the approximate geographical location of the facing. Never sally forth into the turf of a hostile data-target with any files or sensitive documents that you would not want the target to see or to steal. Another good idea, as of getting your files ripped off by the hostiles, is always to keep a hidden stash of duplicate copies of all materials relating to the case (or in the case of photos, and tapes, hide the originals.

Which brings me forward to a worshipful proskynesis at the altar of Lovezap, that term of combative ahimsa or nonviolence, developed by Judith Malina and Julian Beck and the members of the Living Theater, to describe the love energy engendered by highly unified nonviolent direct action. The road of love-zap is ever more productive of good, accurate data than is the road of the pushy investigative goon. And the love-zap path is certainly a great aid in preventing that bane of investigation, the internalization of grouchiness. That is, beware of conducting a personal life as if you were sliding down one of the striations of a garbage grid.

> ahhh sweet love-zap
>   fierce love-zap
>   braced-for-anything love-zap

SECTION III

Presenting Data on the Page
the page is the history
the poem on the page

chant-modes, anapestic/dactylic/choriambic/beowulfian-motorized-
alliterative narratives should be as diverse, in their specific techniques, as the
gene pool o'er which they sing

and the same is true of the poetic adornments of
the page

that is, a page is not a four-sided white void
in which to practice zeroness.

It seems obvious that the language o£ poetry may well evolve into a 1000
color hieroglyphics utilizing a near infinity of typographies. The availability
of colors & photographic images and the 100's of type faces, even in a good
art supply store, foretell the birth of an international hieroglyphics. The
upcoming laser hologram revolution— that is, of 3-dimensional words
& images, speaks and shrieks of a future where poetry and collage and
perspective join to thrill the eye-brain with glowing, animated ("poetry in
motion," the rock-and-roll song so prophetically sang), multi-color, 3-d
"memory gardens" or verse-grids. This new hieroglyphic language may well
use letterless symbols, emotion-glyphs say, 3-d soundless glyphs or tiny
photographs depicting complex emotional states, inserted in the hieroglyphic
grids, to augment the poet's inherited word-horde.

Initially, one can foresee, in a narrative poem say, the use of the protagonists'
"faces" —i.e., small photo-cuts of their faces used *in* the text in place of or in
association with the names. Picture a poem about the relationship of CIA-
director Richard Helms and Robert Kennedy.

In this way, the face-image, by its repetitive appearance in the text, could assume emotional and philosophical qualities; in a Kennedy-Helms poem, the images might emerge as archetypes (and therefore used in other contexts) for baleful secret policeman and for liberal senator.

A list of possible ideas for presentation of verse grids:

a. flow charts—the use of arrows, vector and tensor signs, and specific pictographs to denote relationships, or transformations, or ooze patterns.

b. the use of those headline-making machines one sees in offices of the underground newspapers. A THOUSAND TYPOGRAPHIES for a thousand lines: spatially arranged in beauteous form—what a shame that bards have not brought onward the implications of Apollinaire's *Calligrammes.*

c. the use of mandala-like lyric-wheels, data-wheels, story-wheels as "memory gardens" or as collage/frottage/assemblage thrill farms.

d. One can well study the 1911 collages of Georges Braque, which combined newsprint, paint, wood grains and stone grains, line drawings: giving a sense of equal but multilevel surfaces. Poets could easily borrow some ideas re positioning of verse-grids by studying the prints, say, of Robert Rauschenberg.

e. the Egyptian Soul-Scrolls. These were the long (some as long as three feet) thin rectangular rolls of papyrus placed in the coffin or in the mummy linen of the deceased. The soul-scrolls described in beautifully painted vignettes the arrival and judgement (the weighing of the heart to detect any sin-grime) in the underworld followed by the purification in the lake of fire and then a nice eternity spent picking huge-headed wheat in the Yaru Fields. You can take a look at them in *Mythological* Papyri, Bollingen Series, published by Pantheon, especially vol. 1, facsimiles of the actual soul-scrolls printed on long narrow paper rectangles. They are full of clues regarding the presentation of compressed hieroglyphic poem stories with happy endings.

f. Burroughsian cut-up grids. For information on this read *The Soft Machine*, or any and all of Burroughs' writing on the subject of cut-up techniques.

g. Four or five vertical lines dividing the page, with long narrow verse-columns backed against the lines, in the manner of some of the writing in John Cage's *Silence* (a method of composition used in my own poem, *Cemetery Hill*, which was composed on a page with pre-drawn vertical lines, and the poesy sprayed from my pen up against the lines.)

> Poetry books have seemed to diminish in size of page
> merely to fit the shelf-whims of bookstores. The
> new hieroglyphic verse-grid page will, it seems to me,
> have to be ENLARGED CONSIDERABLY.

> That is, the peripheral space of image presentation
> will have to be enlarged
> whether on larger sheets of paper
> or by using, in not so many years, full-color
> laser verse-fields triggered off by donning
> the latest City Lights Pocket Poets eye-piece.

SECTION IV

Some Observations on the Public Performance of Investigative Poets

It is not an untoward spew of gibberish to predict a "golden age" for the public presentation of verse.

For the same advances that have occurred in meter and method and in hieroglyphic visuality, have also occurred on the electromagnetic front.

Poets will, in the new few years, be able to affix "tone rows" or tangible tone triggers on, say, their forearms, or knees, or thrill-nodes, so that during a poem, merely by touching themselves, they can produce, by beaming signals to a noise-source, concomitant chords, noises, heartbeats, animal songs, percussion, friendly wafts of negative ions, or even projected images that speak in exact harmony (as an overdub in a sound studio, but instanter) with the flow of bard-babble. All parts of a bard's body can be tone-triggers, Patti Smith.

a. The next music: long chanted-or-sung epics or poem-songs (not *song*poems) dealing with current or recent historical events.

b. There will arise the Diogenes Liberation Squadron of Strolling Troubadours & Muckrakers. The likes of Henry Kissinger will tremble before the contrapuntal SO-person chorus of elucidation on the Saturday night Diogenes Strolling Troubadour productions across the country in every natural canyon amphitheatre. Not since the days of Pindar and Sappho, when poems were sung by standing choruses, will such beauty have been heard.

c. The rhabdians— (from wand, ῥάβδος, as mentioned in Olson's *Notes on Language Theatre*: "or single actors w/ a stick beating out verse and acting out narrative situations in said verse, 500 hexameters at a performance, the text the Epics." Apply this to the era of broadcast microphones, tone-triggers, tape loops, etc. and you can guess how some new group of rhabdians might well arise.

d. Tristan Tzara/
       dadaist
    Cafe Voltaire
        poem-operas
            Zurich 1916.

I once observed a "scored sound-opera" for maybe 30 voices, with very professional looking scores written by the composer and performed at the Essen Song festival in Germany, 1968.

An electromagnetic role: Poet as Conductor, or orchestrator of larynxes (of chanting dancers).

(regarding orchestration, a good idea might be to memorize and to internalize various ancient meters, so that, should the occasion occur, you can mix these meters into your natural prosody to produce, say, great pulsing Pindaric choral odes.

e. Investigative Poets to bring about rebirth of the *Ballad Opera*. Motorized Beowulfian recitation of Morality Lists. Rhymed left-wing epics with characterizations played by five-unit choruses.

The tendency of many modern poets also to write songs can come to full fructification in the Ballad Opera.

That is, the ancient image of the Poet as
singer: aoidos (ἀοιδός)
    who carries
    a lyre   φορμίγξ

    Achilles in the Iliad
        sang the kléα ándrών
           (the tunes of men,
              of heroes) (ha ha)
      in the tent

                    & Patrocles
                 is prepared
              to sing too
                    when his
                        turn is come.

              Sort of
                  open poetry
                      readings
           after /before

                    the gore.

But those days of gore-song are done. And we are here to quell the violence, and to return to the ACTUAL TEXTS and MAPS and original languages and modes of culture to find the materials to weave into our public performances.

f. *Howl* as a model for a genre of Indictment Verse. Once again we reiterate how *Howl*, with its long-line iambo-anapestic, bacchic and beat dactylic structure, could easily serve as model for blistering indictments and descriptions of your investigations. Read it a few times and see how it fits: invent melodies for sections of it. Chant it with the percussion, say, of a tambourine as background; practice singing your investigation grids with its long-breath rhythms. If Sappho's unique metre could serve as the basis for a whole school of endeavor, why cannot certain modern poems serve in the same way?

g. Finally, it is probably time for poets to memorize all their poems, especially the partisans of Investigative Poesy, so as to free their arms and hands and bodies to HELP THE PRESENTATION. The triad is this: the spoken text/ the text as beauteously presented on the page/the text as *performed*. Perfection is in the triad.

Do not hesitate to write investigative *songs* (as in Ginsberg's smash CIA-

Calypso song detailing CIA dope-dealing in SE Asia). No one owns the modes. Ahh the modes. Do not hesitate to use every mode that anyone ever devised. The modes of poetry are more powerful than any so-called magic, for they are a proven input. Do not hesitate. Thank you for listening.

CLUE LIST

Some books consulted in preparing this book:

1. *The Complete Poetry of William Blake*. Modern Library Edition.

2. *Blake—Songs of Innocence and Experience*. Introduction by Geoffrey Keynes. Contains reproductions of the painted pages. Oxford University Paperback, 1970.

3. *William Blake & the Age of Revolution,* J. Bronowski, Harper & Row, 1965.

4. *The Poetical Works of Samuel Taylor Coleridge*. Bio-introduction by James Dyke Campbell. London, Macmillan & Co., 1903.

5. Herodotus—*The Histories*.

6. *The Complete Poems and Selected Letters and Prose of Hart Crane*. Edited by Brom Weber. Anchor Books, 1966.
Also, check that fine original edition of *The Bridge*, Horace Liveright, N.Y., 1930.

7. *Encyclopedia Britannica,* 11th edition (purchased for 50¢ at an auction in Kingston, N.Y.) —articles on Coleridge, Wordsworth, Shelley, Pushkin, and particularly Ovid.

8. *Dostoevsky, A Human Portrait*; Robert Payne, N.Y., Alfred A. Knopf, 1961.

9. Also valuable for the history of the agent provocateur: *Cops & Rebels*; Paul Chevigny—hardbound edition published by Pantheon in 1972.

10. Allen Ginsberg
> *Howl and Other Poems*
> *Kaddish*
> *Reality Sandwiches*
> *Planet News*
> *The Fall of America*
>> all from City Lights Books, S.F.
>
> *Ankor Wat* (w/photographs by Alexandra Lawrence, published by Fulcrum Press, London, 1968.

11. *Complete Poetical Works of Percy Bysshe Shelley* (with biographical sketch), Cambridge Edition, 1901, Houghton Mifflin Co.
Shelley: The Pursuit, by Richard Holmes, Dutton, 1975.
Letters of Percy Bysshe Shelley, London Sir Isaac Pitman & Sons, Ltd., 1909.

12. Gary Snyder
> *Earth House Hold*
> *Turtle Island*
>> both New Directions paperbacks.

13. Pushkin, *Selected Verse;* introduction by John Fennell; The Penguin Poets, 1964.

14. Ezra Pound, *The Confucian Odes*, New Directions paperback.
(also, see Olson's book on his visits with Pound after world war 2.)

15. Charles Olson

The Maximus Poems, Jargon/Corinth Books, N.Y., 1960.

Maximus Poems IV, V, VI, Goliard/Grossman, 1968.

Maximus Poems, Volume Three, Grossman, N.Y., 1975.

The Human Universe and Other Essays, Grove Press
1967—contains essay on Projective Verse

Distances, poems by Charles Olson, Grove Press, 1960.

The Selected Writings of Charles Olson, New Directions,
1966.

Poetry & Truth, The Beloit Lectures and Poems, Four
Seasons Foundation, San Francisco, 1971.

*Charles Olson & Ezra Pound: An Encounter at St.
Elizabeth's*, Grossman, 1975.

and valuable as to the specifics: *The Journal of the Charles
Olson Archives*, vols. 1,2,3, edited by George Butterick
and published by the University of Connecticut Library,
Storrs, Conn.

Lightning Source UK Ltd.
Milton Keynes UK
UKHW041816061118
331887UK00001B/148/P